Dec 1999

To Ken, Happy 65th birthday
with love from
        Sarah & Neil
        Jose & Tom.

IMAGES
of England

AROUND

BUDE

GW00584967

Trewin's tailor's shop at Kilkhampton, *c.* 1900, with family and staff. The shop and indeed the business, has long ago disappeared, overcome perhaps by a less formal age and by mass production of clothing.

IMAGES
of England

AROUND

BUDE

Compiled by
Bude, Stratton and District Old Cornwall Society

TEMPUS

First published 1998, reprinted 1999
Copyright © Bude, Stratton and District Old Cornwall Society, 1998

Tempus Publishing Limited
The Mill, Brimscombe Port,
Stroud, Gloucestershire, GL5 2QG

ISBN 0 7524 1120 9

Typesetting and origination by
Tempus Publishing Limited
Printed in Great Britain by
Midway Clark Printing, Wiltshire

Foreword

I can recommend with pleasure this book of photographs and comment about Bude and district. The two compilers, Luc ille Opie and Kenneth Hargrove, take you, for a while, into the recent past of this area in North Cornwall.

Jean Andrew, President
Bude, Stratton and District Old Cornwall Society

Contents

Acknowledgements

The authors are very conscious of their debt to a large number of people who have contributed to the compilation of this book. It is not possible to name them all but the following have loaned precious pictures, offered advice and information from their own researches and generally encouraged us. To them we give our thanks; we are truly grateful. In an enterprise of this nature it is virtually impossible to trace the ultimate origin of all the old pictures and seek permission to use them. We have tried but have not always been successful.

In particular, thanks are due to Peter Truscott, not only for lending pictures but for the knowledge he has imparted about the history of the area. Adrian Abbott and John Stedwill deserve a special mention for their very considerable help; also Don Blizzard, John Bolitho, Bude, Stratton History Museum, Ian Fraser, Des Gregory, Paul Gregory, Joan Heard, Michael Heard, Joan Martin, Ivor Potter, Barrie and Mollie Rose, Julie Shepherd, Carol Smith, George Staddon, Brian Stamp, Margaret Trewin, Bill Young and John Williams.

Introduction

Cornwall's northern coastline is surely unique. Towering and rugged cliffs evoke, with a near mystic quality, inspiration for artist and poet alike. Below them the Atlantic constantly pounds a receding coastline and over the centuries has claimed the lives of many scores of mariners who failed to come to terms with its laws.

The very rocks themselves command another aspect of attraction. Geologists worldwide visit this wild coast to see at first hand how massive internal earth forces have spawned rock formations as weird as they are unusual. On good days this coastline has a majestic but restless beauty unsurpassed by any other part of England, but on bad days the sea can exercise a cruel and unrelenting wilfulness of purposeless destruction.

The villages that shelter in the rare indentations of this rugged coastline are few and far between. In the earlier days sea transport encouraged their survival, since roads and tracks inland were primitive and hazardous. However, in the last hundred years or so these villages have been cosseted by a massive build up of the 'tourist trade'. Bude itself has emerged in such a climate.

The age of a parish church is almost always a guide to the antiquity of the community it serves and Bude is no exception! Its Parish Church of St Michael and All Angels was not built until 1835 and then only as a daughter to the Parish Church of St Andrew at Stratton, which has pre-Norman siting. Stratton was, in fact, a thriving market town commended by Carew in his 1602 *Survey of Cornwall* when Bude was but 'an open sandy bay in whose mouth riseth a little hill by every sea flood made an island'. If Carew's brother-in-law, Master Arundel, had not owned the Manor of Efford, it is doubtful whether Carew himself would ever have bothered to visit Bude at all.

The reasons for the rapid development of the town of Bude and the fall into relative obscurity of Stratton are several and diverse. The building of a canal to carry the sands of Bude Beach to inland farms to temper their acid soils was opened in 1823. This construction included a breakwater and a new sea lock at the town. The railway too, extended from Holsworthy in 1898, used Bude as its terminal, by-passing Stratton altogether. However, the major impetus to growth was the popular acceptance of the idea that total immersion in sea water was not only health giving but immensely pleasurable! Thus Bude in the last century became a much sought and fashionable watering place for the well-to-do. In this century immense social changes and vast developments in transport facilities have changed a sleepy hamlet into a popular tourist resort. Yet while Bude has grown and flourished, the neighbouring village of Stratton has declined into relative obscurity. Whereas in 1802 it boasted twelve alehouses, today that has been reduced to a modest three!

Although Bude itself is essentially a modern town the surrounding area is immensely rich in historical association. In the seventeenth century there was that celebrated gentle giant of Stratton, Anthony Payne, born it is said at Bude and a faithful retainer of Beville Grenville. He fought side by side with Grenville in the latter's last great battle at Lansdowne. Morwenstowe had Hawker, its eccentric vicar-poet of the nineteenth century and Week St Mary's much-married benefactress, Thomasina Bonaventure, who was originally a local shepherdess, became the wife of a Lord Mayor of London. Kilkhampton, 600 feet above sea level, can still show where its Norman castle once stood. To the north of Bude the Grenville family, so prominent in Tudor England, had their great houses and lands at Stowe. To the south the Arundels of Trerice, by judicious marriage had acquired the manor of Efford which eventually became Ebbingford and was inherited by the Acland family of Killerton in the nineteenth century.

There is of course, a great deal more that could be written. In this Cornish peninsula the sea is never very far away and it is in fact the sea that has, over the centuries, exerted its subtle but lasting influence on the character of the people of the Duchy and the conduct of their affairs.

Bibliography

Archaeology of Cornwall, C. Wolf
Bude Canal, H. Harris and M. Ellis
Bude Haven, Captain John Acland
Buildings of Cornwall, W. Pevsner
The Cornish Landscape, W.G.V. Balchin
Cornish Shipwrecks, C. Carter
Cornwall, Jack Ravendale
A Devon Family, Anne Acland
Dictionary of Cornish Place Names, O.J. Padel
Essays on Cornish History, C. Henderson
Histories and Stories of Bude, John Williams
Journals of the Royal Institute of Cornwall
Lake's Parochial History of Cornwall (1974 reprint)
Records of Blanchminster Charity, R.W. Goulding
South West to AD 1000, Malcom Todd
South West England, Aileen Fox
A Survey of Cornwall, R. Carew
The Book of Bude and Stratton, R. Bere and B.S. Stamp
Traveller's Companion to the West Country, M. Jenner
Tudor Cornwall, A.L. Rowse
Vanishing Cornwall, D. du Maurier
Vicar of Morwenstowe, S. Baring-Gould
Wreck and Rescue round the Cornish Coast, Noall and Farr

One
Bude the Town

For close on 400 years Bude had virtually two landlords. The north side of the river Neet was Grenville and later Thynne territory. To the south was Arundel and later Acland land. Both families could trace Norman forbears, and were rewarded after the Civil War for their loyal services to the crown. They lived amicably, co-operating on many projects such as the tidal mill. The real development of the town however was essentially Victorian, speeded along by the opening of the canal in 1832 and accelerated by the arrival of the railway in 1898. Both families took active roles in the extension of the town and were conscious of their responsibilities to the townsfolk. The Aclands concentrated their activities on the Crescent, Breakwater, Killerton and Holnicote roads. They founded Bude's primary school, built the church and granted a benevolent 500 year lease on cliff lands from Compass Point southwards. Meanwhile the Thynnes, from their new home at Penstowe, took an equally active part in the town's development. In 1780 the Bude Hotel, on the present Lloyds Bank site, was built on Thynne land. It was the railway's arrival however, that signalled the real upsurge in their activity. From the Grenville Estate office in Queen Street, Summerleaze Crescent, Morwenna Terrace, Burn View and Queen Street itself were all planned and developed. A vast new hotel on Summerleaze Downs was even planned, though this was never realised on that site.

A view of the Strand with the old bridge, now named after Nanny Moore, who lived in the cottage on the right in the nineteenth century.

Bewd Inn or later, Bude Hotel, was built on land leased by the Thynne family in about 1780. The site was left vacant for many years until the early part of this century. It is now occupied by Lloyds Bank.

This picture was taken around the end of the nineteenth century from the site of the Bude Hotel. It shows the original Globe Hotel and large warehouses along the Strand on the site of the present Strand Hotel.

The Strand, when horse power predominated and life moved at a slower pace. A more modern look is beginning to emerge.

Bellevue in 1929 from the Grenville Hotel, showing Dr King's old home. Dr King was a well known and popular practitioner in the town. The house was later converted to a restaurant and hotel.

Bude Fair before 1903. The first Stratton Fair was sanctioned by a charter from King John at the beginning of the thirteenth century. There were usually two each year, one held at

Whitsuntide and the other at Michaelmas. They were moved from Stratton to Bude in the mid-nineteenth century as the town grew in importance and size.

The Strand in 1920 when the old post office occupied the present National Westminster Bank site.

Blanchminster Square, shown here in 1920, is now the Shute Triangle. Its original name connected it with the famous Blanchminster Charity founded in 1421 and which is still an active organisation. It is the second oldest charity in the country.

The Strand from the Bencoolen Bridge end in about 1880. The Strand has always featured in the life of Bude and, until recent times, was a focus of local activity.

Leven Cot, Nanny Moore's Bridge. The ancient Leven cottages, seen on the left of the bridge, were once a grist (tidal) mill. This picture, taken in 1906, shows the cottage then occupied by the Cobbledick family. On one wall of the cottage there is a granite block inscribed 'AJA 1589', after Anne and John Arundel.

Hartland Terrace was built in the middle of the nineteenth century. Despite the encroachment of the Grenville and Hartland Hotels, some of the original houses still remain.

Bill Oliver's boot and shoe shop was situated on the corner of Bellevue and Princes Street, once the site of the Co-op and now the Merchantman store.

The attractive sweep of the Strand from Bencoolen Bridge to the Triangle has featured in many an album of Bude pictures. This view, taken before 1903, enlivened early Bude holiday guides. The cable running along the Strand came from the Becoolen.

Killerton Road, Bude

Killerton Road was built on Acland land, as the name Killerton implies. It followed the route of an old sheep track to Stratton known as Taggs Lane. Here Messrs Hockin and Banbury's coal cart is making deliveries to the houses of Messrs Arthur and Heard.

Queen Street, with the Grenville Estate office on the left. The street was established by the Thynnes just after the arrival of the railway in 1898, to encourage development in the town.

Bude's third post office was originally on the site of the present National Westminster Bank. It was moved up the hill to an entirely new site in 1928, when this picture was taken at its opening.

A view of Bude from the north west, before the Grenville Hotel was built. Just visible are the upper ends of both Bellevue and Hartland Terrace.

The Parish Church of Bude, dedicated to St Michael and All Angels, was built in 1835 by Sir Thomas Acland on his land above the canal. Initially it was a chapel of ease attached to St Andrews, Stratton, and only became an independent church in 1848. The advowson is now held by the Diocesan Board, thus permitting full local participation in the appointment of the vicar. The church was enlarged in 1876 and again in 1935, just 100 years after its original dedication.

Interior of St Michael's in about 1916, prior to the enlargement. The method of illumination betrays the date of the picture.

503   BUDE FROM SEA

Aerial view of Budehaven showing its location in relation to the Atlantic Ocean and the canal. It clearly demonstrates that Bude is, indeed, a haven on this unfriendly coast where refuge is scarce from Hartland to Padstow.

Telephone : BUDE 140

O. & J. CORY
FAMILY BUTCHERS

Families waited on daily — Only Ox and Heifer Beef supplied
Mechanical killer used — Cold storage

FORE STREET, STRATTON
Your continued Patronage will be appreciated.

S. WICKETT

FAMILY BUTCHER

STRATTON

Phone III

PURVEYOR OF
CHOICE
HOME KILLED MEAT
AND POULTRY

Families waited on Daily
Electrical Refrigerator

W. W. PETHERICK & SONS LTD
Coal and General Merchants, BUDE

QUALITY   Coal, Coke, Anthracite, Logs, Chopped Wood, delivered promptly by Motor Lorries   SERVICE

TELEPHONE 19

This interesting advertisement appeared in the early 1930s when Stratton was still supporting two butchers shops, both promising early deliveries! The lower part shows Petherick's warehouse, which was on the upper canal basin. It has now been replaced by residential apartments.

Legg's wheelwrights shop was on the upper wharf at the bottom of Lynstone Road. From the right are father Henry (born in 1831 in Stratton), with sons Ernie, Fred and Jack. This later became Gregory's the blacksmith.

Gregory's gate. The original William Gregory, who ran the foundry on the upper wharf at the end of the last century, is displaying with legitimate pride a piece of his wrought iron craftsmanship.

Hussey's greengrocery business was set up by George Hussey in 1893 and continued until after the First World War. Although goods were largely displayed outside, there was provision for combating the elements. The premises eventually became part of Woolacott's electrical and radio shop.

A picture of Bellevue showing Underwood's store, taken much later than the one below. In the same block are Lennards, Cornish Stone and Isaac's the optician. Those were the days when one could drive down Bellevue as well as up!

Bude Riding Stables occupied part of Springfield Cottage at the top of Bellevue. This was the home of Monty Thorn, a carriage proprieter.

When Othello Terrace was demolished, Dr Arthur King built and occupied Grosvenor House on the site. It later became a hotel, then a china shop. The car is parked in Hartland Terrace opposite.

N.J. Hawking and Son's store on the corner of Lansdowne Road and Queen Street. This picture from 1930 shows Nicholas James Hawking junior, the son of the founder of the business which eventually became N.E. Truscott Bude Ltd. In Mr Hawking's day the shipping agency was a significant part of the business.

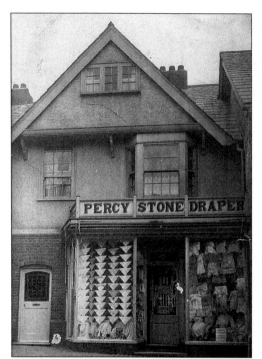

Amongst the earlier commercial denizens of Princes Street were Daymans and Percy Stone. Daymans (below) ran a gentleman's tailoring and ladies' costumery and millinery shop whilst Percy Stone had an extensive drapery business. Both shops now form part of Keat's stores.

The original Keat's shop in Princes Street with sundry ironmonger's wares outside.

Mr G. Tucker was a butcher and poulterer who occupied premises in upper Bellevue next to the riding stables. As can be seen from the picture he kept a fine variety of merchandise!

Looking across Summerleaze Beach in 1900, the Grenville Hotel had not yet been built.

Glenville Hotel, Bude

The original intention was to build the Grenville Hotel on Summerleaze Downs close to the cricket field. After a bitter public battle the project was dropped and the present site well away from the Downs was chosen. It opened in 1912. One of the original advertisements read 'Largest hotel facing the Atlantic seaboard'. This hotel has now become the Adventure International.

Messrs Hockin and Banbury were agricultural and general merchants. The term 'general' covered such diverse commodities as timber, coal and a multiplicity of building materials. They also traded in wool. Mr G.W. Banbury, a son, sold the business to Messrs Fulford's in 1923. It has now been acquired by Travis Perkins and is situated in the lane behind. Wroe and Briggs were pioneers in the field of wireless when 'wet batteries, grid bias and valves that lit' ruled the day. Furse and Jones butchers will be remembered by some Bude residents as the shop where mother bought the Sunday joint.

Fred Staddon ran the forge and farriers on the canal repairing all the iron work on the lock gates and the like; George Bickle did the leather work and Sab Curtis made the wagons and wheels. Fred was also responsible for the metal 're-enforcment' in the construction of the Summerleaze bathing pool. This building now houses the Bude Museum.

BATHERS

WILL BE ALLOWED TO USE THE
NEW BATH POOL,

at the end of the Breakwater, while Canvass is set up for Shelter, on paying **2d.** *each time for attendance, to the man in charge of the Pool.*

Canvass will be set (weather permitting) half an hour before half ebb Tide, and be kept up as may be found convenient and desirable until about half an hour after half flood Tide.

By consent of the Bude Harbour and Canal Company, and of the Lord of the Manor of Efford.

For further Information apply to Mr. GEORGE HEARD, Post Office, Bude Haven.

BUDE HAVEN, 1859.

The Bathing Pit, Bude

205373 J.V

Tommy's Pit. (See below)

Opposite: The French Revolution and the wars in Europe forced many well-to-do families to seek alternatives to fashionable Continental watering places for their summers. Cornwall was an obvious choice. In Bude Sir Thomas Acland, who had inherited the Manor of Efford when 16 years old, recognised its potential and built not only a summer residence for his family and friends, but also developed facilities, including the Falcon Hotel, to attract visitors to enjoy a seaside holiday. The arrival of the railway at Bude connected the Atlantic seaboard with the Capital and this accelerated and diversified the tourist trade. Sea bathing 'total immersion' developed as a popular pastime of the wealthy during the late nineteenth century. It was encouraged in Bude by Sir Thomas Acland who built Tommy's Pit at the end of the breakwater. This was Bude's first bathing pool but was strictly for gentlemen. It was 'graduated in depth for their convenience'. Ladies had exclusive use of Maer Beach, now Crooklets. There was no mixed bathing until after the First World War.

33

Bude's open air swimming pool, built in 1930 on Summerleaze Beach, is essentially a tidal pool with a sea lock. Colonel Thynne saved the original project by agreeing to meet half the cost. Fred Staddon at the Old Smithy was responsible for producing the interlocking metal strips visible in the picture. These long strips had to be hooked together and concreted quickly, the builder co-ordinating his work with the tides.

BUDE. THE BATHING POOL. 69839

Bude bathing pool in the late thirties shows popular holiday attire of the day. Note both the gentleman in plus fours and some of the millinery creations. The children's pool on the left no longer exists.

Opposite: When this picture was taken in 1930 the law did not allow changing on the beach, most people still sought a little privacy, although the bathing huts did not have to be dragged to the water's edge as both ladies and gentlemen insisted they did in Victorian times.

The petrified forest can be seen at Crooklets Beach on both the north and south sides. Exposed rarely, due to high tides and shifting sands, the wood appears to be black rock until touched.

Summerleaze Beach had a very different appearance in 1926 with its old fashioned tea room, beach huts differently positioned and, of course, a car park had not yet been constructed.

In pre-war Britain family fun on holiday meant sunshine, sea, sand and donkeys. Bude offered them all, with wonderful cliff walks for good measure.

Bude's first picture house was built by a Walsall businessman, Robert Edgar Booth, in 1922. It stood on the corner of Burn View opposite what is now the Co-op. Somewhat optimistically the founders planned seating for 600, despite the fact that the entire population of Bude was then only 3,000. One of the first feature films shown was *The Hound of the Baskervilles*, silent of course, but with the appropriate musical accompaniment.

To introduce the film *Aces High* the cinema owner, Mr David Burkey, gave a sherry party. Seen with him are Council Chairman C.W. Ellicott, Mr W. Gregory, who had served in the Royal Flying Corps and a German aviator.

Opposite: The New Picture House, built on the edge of the Downs at the top of Bellevue, was opened in 1936. Sadly, due to economic problems it closed in 1985. The site is now occupied by a supermarket.

Two examples of the enterprise of Capt Brinton. Above, he is operating his ferry from Summerleaze Beach across the river at high tide. Below is the pontoon bridge which he set up at low tide. Although the ladies appear apprehensive, *Rover* is clearly enjoying the fun!

Compass Point is one of the most impressive natural features of the Bude coastline and the Storm Tower which adorns it was built and paid for by Sir Thomas Acland, *c.* 1823. For many years it served as the local coast guard station. The Tower is a unique octagonal building designed ingeniously with slits to permit all round observation of shipping yet protecting the observer. In the 1880s it was moved back from the cliff edge because of coastal erosion, a constant threat to Cornwall's north coast. The compass points are now several degrees out of true, possibly due to the variation of the magnetic field.

This animated scene at Bude Fair in 1907 was caught by the camera in what was then Blanchminster Square, now the Triangle. It seems that the general high spirits that fairs generate has changed but little - only the way people dress is different!

Opening a new sewage works in 1909 hardly seems a cause for general rejoicing, but this one in Bude was an enormous step forward from the arrangements that previously existed, ie. 'earth closets'! The ceremony was held at the sewer's Efford Down 'trap' just south of the Storm Tower.

The Silver Jubilee of King George V and Queen Mary in 1935 was an occasion for celebrations in Bude. Here are the revellers in King Street, which has been suitably 'dressed' for the occasion!

Opposite: The opening of the new open air swimming pool on Summerleaze Beach in 1930 was greeted with great local satisfaction - not least that it had been achieved at all! Included here, amongst others, are Mrs Constance Thynne, Sir Francis Acland and Mr Jeffries.

This view of the present Lansdown Road was taken in the 1950s and shows Smales' grocery store in the middle. Of particular interest is the pillar box which marks Bude's first mail collection centre, it was then No.1 Garden Terrace. The wall and garden have long since gone and the present post box is free standing.

Bude celebrated Empire Day in 1906 with a grand parade of the Duke of Cornwall's Light Infantry and a concert by the band. They are seen outside the Drill Hall, now the Neetside Centre.

44

A slate plaque was placed on the Castle Wall in 1977 to commemorate Bude's association with that well known Cornish inventor and innovator, Sir Goldsworthy Gurney. Gurney, amongst other things, built Bude Castle, lit the House of Commons and was largely responsible for the adoption of a standard time throughout England. The plaque was presented by Bude, Stratton Old Cornwall Society and in this picture are Mesdames Bennett, Martin and Usher, Miss Venning and Messrs Heard and Spencer Howlett.

Bristol's Clifton College was evacuated to Bude during the Second World War to escape the German air raids, and a Commemoration Stone was set on Summerleaze Downs to mark the event. It was unveiled in 1968 by Chairman of the Council Mr Eric Chadd, seen here with his wife and members of staff and of the Council.

This splendid picture of the Great Blizzard of 1891 was taken in what is now the Triangle at the bottom of Lansdown Road. It is easy to see why this particular snowstorm has earned a place in Bude legend.

Children on Summerleaze Beach in the snow, in the early sixties.

The 'freeze up' of 1963 was an awesome one and these pictures of skating on the canal and Flexbury Church bear witness to its severity.

Castle and cottages looking across the route of the old Causeway probably before the wreck of the Bencoolen which was in 1862. The recreation ground now lies between them.

The Bude Recreation Ground which was created by private enterprise in 1923 and provides for both visitors and residents, with bowls, squash and tennis facilities.

Floods have been endemic to Bude for a long time. There are early records of flooding in 1846 and again in 1876, but there have been many more intrusions that have gone unrecorded except in the memories of the victims. Destruction of sandhills, building a breakwater, the joining of Chapel Rock to the mainland and the general reconstruction associated with the canal and sea lock no doubt exacerbated the problem. A bore build-up with the spring tides induces rapid rises in river level. When this coincides with heavy rainfall and high winds the effects can be disastrous for the town. It is fair to say that the considerable efforts made to reduce the problem have met with some success, but the elements, working in unison, are a formidable combination and hard to master.

Records indicate that the flooding of 1903 was particularly bad, but, as these pictures show
Bude, suffered equally in other years

All flood pictures tend to look alike and these, taken in 1993, the last year of serious flooding, look very much like their predecessors. In that year the newly built Parkhouse Centre was put out of commission for several months and occupants of the Crescent were forced to take refuge in upper rooms until rescued by boat. The Harris's bridal party had an unusual ride to the church through the sterling efforts of the R.N.L.I.

St Petroc's School, Downs View, now the Eventide Residential Home. The co-founders were the Misses Ethel Cherrill and Anne Vivian, and the school originally occupied premises in Killerton Road, now St Margaret's Hotel. Initially there were three boarders, two day boys and three dogs! By January 1918 a move to larger premises became essential due to rising numbers. Then in 1926 a further move was made from Downs View to Ocean View Road where it has remained ever since. Its record of achievement, both scholastic and sporting, is a worthy tribute to the vision and memory of its founders.

In this 1923 photograph are the Misses Vivian, Cherrill and Miss 'Steve', later the wife of the redoubtable J. Zambra who served the school for forty-six years and who will be remembered for his propensity to shorts, winter and summer! In the background is Spencer Howlett, then a scholar, a founder member of Bude Old Cornwall Society, who remained its secretary for many years.

Founded in 1938, Stratton Secondary School marked the beginning of the building programme for the reorganisation of education in Cornwall. Pupils were sent to one of the secondary schools from the surrounding primary schools and some children had a considerable distance to travel. The catchment area having a twenty-five mile radius, transport and a midday meal had to be provided. The two secondary schools were functional until the arrival of the new building for comprehensive education in the 1980s. Stratton Secondary School has now become the primary school for Stratton.

The old Bude Junior School was founded in 1851 by Sir Thomas Acland. It was a charity school (a school for the poor) and was controlled by the Church of England. There are records that state that a Henry B. Williams was the schoolmaster of the Charity School in 1841 to1844 and of the new school in 1851. One penny a week was charged so that both boys and girls could master the basics of English and Arithmetic. They were rarely able to attend after the age of ten because they would have to work for their living! When Bude's new junior school was built at the top of Broadclose Hill, it was acquired by the local council and now serves as a civic focal point, renamed the Parkhouse Centre.

Bude Grammar School was founded in 1909 at Bramble Hill, Pathfields, and had sixty pupils. They were sent from the surrounding primary schools which had been, up till then 'all age' schools. The members of staff in 1963 from top left are: R. Morgan, A. Harris, E. Baker, M. Chegwin, F. Worral (headmaster), B. Wright, J. Thomas, J. Davies, I. Davies, A. Martin, D. Williams, H. Martin. Front row: P. Holdcroft, P. Green, G. Rees, M. Kelly and V. Tilzey.

Two
Bude and the Sea

'But a time it comes to ships and men, when sailing days are past,
Even such as hail from Devon, where they mostly build to last.
And her seams began to open and the Severn tide came through,
And the water kept on gaining spite of all they could do.'
(Blue Peter, C. Fox Smith, 1937)

Efford Cottage, built in the 1820s by Sir Thomas Acland, was used as a summer residence for his family and friends. It remained Acland property until the Second World War. The site had previously been a fisherman's cottage, latterly used for salting fish.

Steps have now been provided to climb Chapel Rock and records indicate that the Rock housed a small medieval chapel dedicated to St Michael. When the canal was built Chapel Rock was joined to the mainland by a breakwater. The sea is unusually calm.

Bude Canal sea lock before 1900, showing the sea lock entrance at low tide.

A contemporary picture of sailing ships approaching the lock as the tide rises. Note the Hobbler's Hut, centre, with the chimney pointing skywards!

A ship in the lower basin of the canal with the river in the foreground and Chapel Rock on the horizon.

In 1924 Petherick's warehouse on Sir Thomas Acland's wharf on the south side of the canal's upper basin was a hive of activity. Here four motor lorries are visible but only one horse-drawn coal cart, a sign of changing times.

The ketch *Traly* was for some time owned and operated by W.W. Petherick of Bude. Built in 1912, she was still sailing in Baltic waters in 1990.

SS Rushlight, seen here in Bude Canal in 1923, was one of the very few genuine 'steamers' to unload in the basin.

This memorable picture taken in 1897 shows the lower basin of Bude Canal crowded with ships. On the left are: *Elizabeth* (Capt Brinton); *Sir T. Acland* (Capt Hallett); *Purveyor* (Capt Rook); *Traly* (Capt Mountjoy); *Hawk* (Capt Martin); *Lady Acland* (Capt Cunningham); *Boconnoc* (Capt Sluggett); *Kindly Light* (Capt J.B. Cook). The vessels on the right are: *Friendship* (Capt Stephens); *Ant* (Capt Hines); *Brackley* (Capt Morgan); *Joseph & Thomas* (Capt Shazel); *Stuckley* (Capt Cook); *Wild Pigeon* (Capt Barrett); *Ceres* (Capt Petherick); *Do I Win* (Capt Chidgey).

This tranquil picture taken around the turn of the century shows the lower reaches of the canal before the railway was extended to the lower wharf. This extension proved the death knell of the canal as a commercial artery. The Crescent can be seen behind the marshes.

The original breakwater (above), reproduced from a sketch by Sir Thomas Acland, was built in 1823 and succumbed to the elements fifteen years later. An interesting, if vulnerable, feature was the circular tower at the sea end. This was not replaced on the second breakwater (below). The present structure, which is 4 ft lower, has a gentler sea slope but is the same length as its predecessor - about 830 ft.

Above: Unloading coal from the ketch *Traly* into Bill Short's cart on the lower wharf about 1936. On deck holding the rope is Jack Bowden of Appledore. There is evidence to suggest the horse was called *Lion*!

Below: These mile posts (left) were placed in 1831 along the canal tow path and some can still be seen. Tub boats, equipped with wheels to surmount inclined planes, were originally designed for use on the upper part of the canal above Hele Bridge. As the right picture shows, latterly some migrated to the lower basin, seen here with the *Stucley* of Padstow. Tub boats could carry about 5 tons of sand.

The first of Bude's three swing bridges was built in 1820. The present permanent structure was opened in 1962, making the upper basin inaccessible to shipping. Above, the second wooden construction of 1887 was designed to permit the passage of the lifeboat. It was replaced in 1906 by a much more robust iron structure, seen below in its open position, with some of its construction crew aboard.

Hele Bridge, Marhamchurch, is two miles from the sea. This bridge, still in existence, though no longer on the main road, was built around 1820.

The first lock on the canal was at Rodd's Bridge and was 63 ft long and 14 ft wide, raising the canal by 5 ft 6 ins.

The prevailing wind on the north Cornish coast is from the south west which means that should power fail, be it sail or mechanical, a ship will be driven inevitably onto a rocky and possibly inhospitable shore. Over the centuries tales of wrecks, wreckers, heroism and skullduggery have become part of Bude history and Cornish legend. This photograph shows wreckage from the *SS Bencoolen*. Disaster struck the Indiaman on 21 October 1862 when, pounded by heavy seas, she became a total wreck on Summerleaze Beach. Twenty-nine of the crew of thirty-five were lost. Bude still has a bridge and a road named after this famous tragedy. Law enforcement officers of the day can be seen standing guard over a massive pile of wreckage.

In October 1899 a north westerly gale blew the SS *Llandaff* ashore. The crew of eleven were rescued during the storm by breeches-buoy before the ship came to rest above the old swimming pool (known as Tommy's Pit). She was eventually refloated and towed to Cardiff.

Opposite: Ketch *President Garfield* left Bude in ballast on 14 March 1906. When the wind fell she drifted ashore north of the entrance to the harbour. This view shows the Bude lifeboat making its successful attempt to rescue the crew.

The *Elizabeth* under Summerleaze Point in February 1912, with the lifeboat in attendance.

This is believed to be the *Hawk* stranded off Summerleaze at the beginning of the century, watched by crowds from the cliff top.

Above is the SS *Belem* ashore at Northcott Mouth in November 1917 with a cargo of iron ore. The crew walked ashore at low tide but the ship was a total wreck and was scrapped where she lay. The lower picture, taken in 1997, tells the tale of eighty years of Atlantic pounding!

The third lifeboat to be stationed at Bude (*Elizabeth Moore Garden 2*) is seen alongside the *The Brackley* at anchor in Bude Harbour, *c*. 1897.

Bude's maritime Methuselah, the ketch *Ceres*, probably the best known of all Bude vessels, traded regularly with Bristol Channel ports. She was 125 years old when she foundered off Baggy Point in 1936 and for eighty-four of those years she was owned, and for a good part sailed, by the Petherick family.

The first lifeboat to be installed at Bude was in 1837, ordered by King William IV, and manned by untrained crews of coast guards, fishermen, sailors and others who happened to be around and who would volunteer! (Hardly satisfactory, but they did their best) In 1863 a new boat was launched. It was housed by the canal basin on land provided by Sir Thomas Acland. She was named the *Elizabeth Moore Garden* after her benefactress and saved many lives from 1863 to 1886. This view shows the lifeboat house on the canal just above the Falcon Bridge in 1890, with a crew assembled ready to harness up a team of horses. The new lifeboat bore the same name as her predecessor, the *Elizabeth Moore Garden 2*.

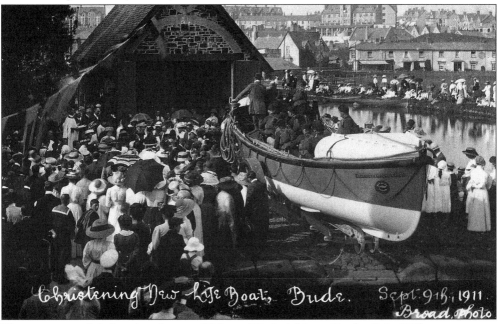

The ceremony of christening the new lifeboat, *Elizabeth Moore Garden 3*, in 1911.

A team of horses dragging the lifeboat (*Elizabeth Moore Garden 2*) into deep water so that the crew could take over. The boat was launched stern first to protect the rudder.

Lifeboat exercising off Maer Beach, regular practice being an integral part of the lifeboat man's job.

R.N.L.I. Lifeboat Day in 1906, celebrated with a procession led by the Town Band, seen marching along the Crescent towards Bencoolen Bridge.

Celebration of R.N.L.I. Day in 1907, included an umbrella race in the canal, but not for the faint hearted!

When the French Pit Wood dandy *Jeannot* foundered off Millook in 1919 the crew were rescued by breeches-buoy as the lifeboat was unable to reach the ship. A rocket fired across the ship carried a line which secured the breeches-buoy and enabled members of the crew to be brought ashore.

The crew of the ketch *Traly* in the late 1930s. From the left are: F. Clark, W. Ford, Alfred Petherick and O. Jeffrey. The *Traly*, built in 1912, was purchased by the Pethericks as a replacement for the *Ceres* which foundered in 1936.

In 1966, under a new R.N.L.I. rescue policy, an inshore rescue boat and station were commissioned at Bude. Some of the people seen here with Canon Walter Prest dedicating the lifeboat include: Mr and Mrs Howlett, Mr and Mrs Ridler, W. Whately, J. Turner, B. Jorden, N. Pepperell and G. Moorish.

The ancient ceremony of Blessing the Sea was revived in Bude in the 1920s. The service was attended by all denominations and conducted at Ocean Caves near the breakwater.

The arrival of the railway in 1898 put paid to the canal's commercial activities, but the sea lock, of course, operated for considerably longer. The upper picture shows a placid holiday scene when the lower wharf had been almost totally abandoned by shipping. Below we see the canal's transition to a popular leisure area for boating enthusiasts and fishermen. The scene is near the first lock at Rodds Bridge. Both were taken in the early 1930s.

Three
Coaches and Railways

The Turnpike Acts of 1760 and 1792 set in motion immense improvements in the county's road system and in so doing, ushered in the great age of coaching. New roads were planned to follow river valleys and Bude took a prominent part in that exciting era. A Coombe's Guide of the mid-nineteenth century for instance, reveals the astonishing fact that there were at that time three alternative ways of getting to London, each one commencing with a coach ride to rail heads at Barnstaple, Okehampton or Launceston!

This photograph was taken in about 1896 outside Bray's shop at the end of the Strand, now Nat West corner. The Parish Hall, built in 1894, is just visible in the background. Looking at the picture a team of four may have been hard pressed to pull that load up Old Stratton Hill!

Nineteenth century Bude was a busy coaching centre and there were at least four operators in the town. This picture was taken in about 1900 outside the Falcon Hotel, from where George Brendon operated his coaches.

Passengers are aboard and ready to move off from outside the London South Western booking office in the Strand, Bude, c. 1898. The coach driver is William ('Bill) Wonnacott.

This famous picture of Ned Sherrick and *Snowball*, with the Falcon horse bus outside Bude station was probably taken prior to the First World War. Before the railway arrived at Bude the horse bus travelled as far as Holsworthy to meet the train.

Another coaching departure point was the Carrier's Inn, previously called The Inn on the Strand. A Miss Cobbledick was the proprietress when this picture was taken.

After immense local pressure the railway was finally extended from Holsworthy to the Atlantic seaboard at Bude in 1898. The railway's arrival had far reaching effects. It virtually ensured the demise of Stratton, which it by-passed; hastened the decline of coastal trade; and opened up Bude to the rapidly growing tourist trade. Above is the main platform as it appeared a couple of years after the grand opening, when all the triumphal arches had been removed. Below, a collection of horse carriages await the arrival, perhaps, of the Waterloo express. Bude coaches were detached at Exeter and the whole journey from London in the 1930s could take under 5 hours without changing coaches.

These two pictures show the line of the extension of the railway to Bude Quay and the salt water lock with a freight train actually crossing the main road near the Falcon Bridge. The canal as a commercial artery thus became a thing of the past.

Bude station in the 1920s. Bude, the Southern Railway's Atlantic terminal at this time, was well equipped with a book stall, a waiting room and its own signal box, as well as a modern goods depot with adequate facilities for shunting etc.

A passenger train arriving from Exeter. The Southern Railway's Atlantic terminal at Bude was a busy spot, particularly on Saturdays in summer!

Bude's rail link with Okehampton came under the 'Beeching Axe' thus ending nearly 70 years of service. The last train, seen standing at the main platform, was a very different mechanical conveyance to the steam monster that had opened the line with such panoply in 1898.

On high days and holidays in summer during the early 1920s, a motor-coach ran from Bude to Boscastle and Tintagel. Here it is outside Bray's shop in the Strand, at a time when the internal combustion engine was still an exciting innovation.

The staff of Bude station in 1898 in the railway's halcyon days soon after it opened. At the centre back is Mr Thomas Full the stationmaster with daughters Gertie and Lily in front and, to his left, Charles Furze. The bowler-hatted figure kneeling is Jack Smale, driver of the Holsworthy mail cart. Seated is Fred May, driver of the Holsworthy coach. On the extreme right is Mr Burnard, goods guard, and the smartly dressed passenger guard is Mr Woodcock. The bearded gentleman is Jim Abbott with porter Harry Berryman and two others standing in front.

Four
Historic Homes

The political stability and prosperity of Tudor England hastened the transition from a fortified residence for protection, to the 'stately home', where comfort, privacy and excellent architectural design became more important. Fine examples of this revolutionary type of house building can be seen throughout the length and breadth of Cornwall and the Bude area is no exception.

Bertha Stamp's excellent drawing of Ebbingford Manor, or 'Efford'. This was once the property of the Arundel family of Trerice and was inherited by Sir Thomas Acland at the beginning of the century. He presented it to Bude to be used as St Michael's Vicarage. In 1954 it became the home of Sir Dudley Stamp, the eminent geographer.

Efford Down House, built in 1848, was the home of Arthur Mills, Sir Thomas Acland's son-in-law, one time MP for Taunton and Exeter. The house was a wedding present to Agnes and Arthur from Sir Thomas.

Stowe Barton in 1885. Although the mighty Grenvilles flourished in Tudor times, all that now remains above ground of the two Grenville houses at Stowe near Kilkhampton is the converted stable block of the Earl of Bath's Restoration mansion. It is now the property of the National Trust and operates as a farm house.

-*Bude's Forgotten Genius*-

SIR GOLDSWORTHY GURNEY
1793-1875

Although Sir Goldsworthy Gurney (right) was born in Padstow, he spent a great deal of his adult life in Bude and is in fact buried in Launcell's churchyard. His fertile imagination, engineering skill and entrepreneurial spirit, in a word - genius, were well suited to his times. After building Bude Castle with enormous ingenuity on a sand base he found his wife did not like it and they moved to Reeds at Poughill (below). He lived here with his elder daughter, Anna Jane, after his wife's death. Anna Jane presented a clock to Poughill Church in memory of this forgotten genius.

Penfound Manor, near Poundstock, is reputed to be one of the oldest manor houses in England and stands on the site, according to Domesday, of a fortified manor house once the property of Edward the Confessor's Queen. Vestiges of the Saxon walls can be traced in the structure. The Penfound family, whose political judgement was notoriously faulty (and who paid for it!) lived in the manor from the fourteenth to the eighteenth centuries; the last known Penfound died in 1847. In the present century much patient and scholarly restoration has been attempted. One of the triumphs must surely be the re-emergence of the medieval Great Hall (below left). This view (above) of the south frontage in the sunshine of an earlier summer, after roofs, porch and chimney stacks had been restored, illustrates the grace and serenity of this ancient house. The 'Elizabethan' staircase, (below right) - surely Jacobean - has remained virtually unchanged since the eighteenth century.

A porch was added by Arthur and Sibella Penfound in 1643. The date is carved across the top of the arch and the letters 'A.S.' can just be seen on the left spandiel, whilst the letter 'P' is on the right of the granite arch.

PENFOUND MANOR, THE PORCH

Possibly dating from Saxon times, the ancient manor of Tonnacombe, originally called Tidnacombe Manor, is mentioned in a terrier dated 1296. The present manor house north of Bude is a very fine example of sixteenth century architecture, including, as it does, many of the original features. The restoration of the minstrel gallery was recorded by Parson Hawker and the splendid oak panelling is attributed to the Kempthorne family, who were resident in the late sixteenth century. In the grounds a stone survival may be the remains of a Cornish Cross. The house is a private residence.

The Falcon at Bude is one of the oldest and most prestigious coaching inns in north Cornwall. Opened in 1798 and now a three star hotel, it was run by the Brendon family for over 100 years, and has entertained the great and the good, including Alfred Tennyson and Earl Mountbatten. This view, around 1880, shows the hotel before the addition of the tower and the general extension of 1912.

The Bullers Arms, Marhamchurch, taken in 1928, has an interesting association with the well known Buller family of Crediton, Devon. General Redvers Buller, a prominent member of that family, was very much involved in South African military campaigns.

Five
Bude Folk

It is the people who make social history. There is a wide variety of clubs and organisations in the area, some of which were founded in the late nineteenth century and many are surviving today. The following pictures show a number of Bude people that should help readers recall some of Bude's social history!

A contingent of the Duke of Cornwall's Light Infantry entering Bude in 1908, headed by Bude Band.

This picture of a charming milkmaid on her rounds complete with float, churns and compliant horse, was taken in the 1920s, a time when milk bottles were a rarity and milk arrived on the doorstep daily

Messrs Hockin and Banbury's main buildings stood on the site of the present Strand Hotel. The public entrance was on the Strand, with warehouse access and a large yard behind.

Crew of the ketch *Alford*. From the left: J. Cooper, H. Hines (jun), H. Hines, N. Penfound and G. Perry. It is not known when this picture was taken, but it was probably before 1918.

Coastguard exercise at Upton in 1947, showing Mr Sydney Stewart, the Chief Coastguard Officer of Bude Station with the District Senior Officer.

The retirement of Wilf Whateley from the R.N.L.I. (seated in front) in 1985 after thirty-seven years service. Back row, from left to right are: Messrs Ian Whitfield, Jan Petherick, Colin Jeffery, Bob Thomas, Tim Marshall, Bill Cloke, Jon Ball, Keith Perkins, Peter ?, Eric Seymour, Patrick Shelley. Front row: Paddy Frost, Des Gregory, Mike Moyle, Pat Whateley, Wilf Whateley, John Thorn, Derek Ridler and Dr David Giles.

An outing of Bude Girl Guide Company on 15 May 1945 or 1946, shortly after the end of the Second World War.

Bude County School mixed tennis finalists in 1950. From left to right: T. Pickard, N. Dodd, Dr Long (headmaster), P. Mossman, S. Thorn and L. Tozer.

Pupils from Stratton Secondary School made an adventurous trip to London in 1954. Accompanying them were three members of staff. Mr Lloyd Sweet and Miss Betty Newman are in the back row and Mr Tony Grimshaw is on the right of the picture.

The Comprehensive School's new buildings for the upper school were *in situ* in 1973. The lower half still used the old Stratton School buildings for several years after. Some of the pupils, staff and parents are seen here setting out on a European trip to Amsterdam by coach in 1977.

Bude soccer team in 1948. Back row, from left to right: J. Day, T. Rickard, W. Keat, Topsy Burrows, D. Oke, Tubby Gilbert. Front row: L. Tozer, Taffy Williams, K. Aunger, G. Martin and J. Reynolds.

Bude Cricket Club became the North Cornwall Cricket Club in 1958. This picture was taken at the inauguration celebrations. From left to right: Messrs Shobrook, -?-, T. Pickard (chairman of the council), M. Cole, D. May, C. Pickard, J. Tilsey, D. Ridler, L. Sweet, -?-, -?-, I. Opie, E. Stanbury, B. Walton, D. Heywood, M. Cann, T. Grimshaw.

The Bude and North Cornwall Golf Club was founded in 1891, the Summerleaze Downs being leased from the local landowner Mr F.J. Thynne. Despite early fears that golf might be just a passing phase, it very quickly became successful and was an added attraction to Bude as a fast-growing holiday resort. Of course in the early days it had 'Artisan v. Gentlemen' as well as 'Right of Way' problems! However, all that is history and today golf is played and enjoyed by all sections of the community and visitors alike. It is fortunate indeed that the course was set out in those early days before the town developed, as it prevented the beautiful Downs becoming a built up area. Above: The Ladies Gammon Cup winners (1985?) were, back row, from left to right: Sally Willis, Kathy Keat, Joan Sandon, Pat Clark, Sue Cann. Front row: -?-, Peggy Cann, Liz Willis, Morwenna Abbott, Millie Clare. In the veteran's team (below) in the late 1980s were, standing from left to right: Percy Curtis, Alf Tilley, Jim Misercough, George Staddon, Frank Clark, Hanz Schubert, Courtney Pickard, Lesley Lea, Ernie Yeo, George de Jon and Fred Brabham. Front row: Nick Chadfield, Harry Downs, Jack Clare and Fred Heard.

Bude Carnival 1954. Ivy Joll and friends remind us that Henry VIII had six wives!

Jollification at the New Year's Ball for the Bude Squash Club, held at the Grenville Hotel, 1962(?). This hotel was a very popular venue for dinner-dances during the early part of this century.

The County Bowling Championships in 1954 when Cornwall opposed Nottingham with the Grenville Hotel in the background.

Bude Rugby Club's First XV, 1970/1. Back row, from left to right: Neck, Schiller, Troke, Boundy, Risden, Willoughby, Petherick, Wickett, Rees, Opie. Front row: Hicks, Stephens, Harris, Poulton, Tilzey, Edwards, Smith and Orchard.

Bude's Surf Life Saving Club, the first in Britain, was formed in 1953 by an Australian, Alan Kennedy and a local man, Peter Cloke. Above are the team in that first year with Alan Kennedy MBE. From left to right: G. Mill, J. Legg, R. Wellington, T. Lashbrook, M. Martin, F. Lester, A. Kennedy, G. Hutchinson (youth leader), P. Cloke, L. Wellington, A. Brock, P. Martin and A. May. Below: the presentation in 1955 when Bude won the National Championships. The Australian, Colin Hendy (past president) presents the cup to Peter Cloke. Behind them, from the left are: Mike Martin, Robin Wellington, Glyn Mill, Gavin Sampson and Richard Cloke. Peter was awarded the BEM for his services to Surf Life Saving.

Bude Surf Life Saving Club Ladies Team, 1965, all looking very healthy and beautiful! From the left: Heather Wroe, Carol Adams, Denise House, Christine Green, Elizabeth McMahon and Patricia Taylor.

Budehaven Tennis Club was formed in 1923 by some Bude business people. Although there was already a lawn tennis club, only the gentry were allowed to join! A piece of land was purchased on the old Causeway, now the Recreation Ground, and a board of directors set up to run it. Today tennis is very popular and the club thrives. Seen here are club members in 1947 when the club resumed activities after the Second World War. Amongst those present are: Margaret Clowes, Ron Thorn, Margaret Kelly, Trevor May, Phyllis Cloke, M. Howard, Mary McCabe and Ruth John.

The year 1923 marked the end of an era for the Bude Lifeboat Station when it closed down after nearly a century. Seen here is the well known coxwain of the fifth lifeboat *Elizabeth Moore Garden 3*, Mr Barrett, in 1920.

The Bude Fire Brigade at the Wharf. The group includes Jack Parkhouse (third from left) who was a member of the well known Parkhouse family, benefactors of Bude.

During the Second World War the fire service was handled with efficiency, success and charm by the distaff side. Back row, from left to right: Eddy, Williams, Bate, Lupton, Langdon and Evans. Front row includes: Skinner, Lyle, King, Oxenberry and Yeo.

Procession of Bards crossing Nanny
Moore's Bridge, 1961.

Councillor Eric Trewin welcomes the
Bards in the castle grounds in 1975.

The Lady of Cornwall, Miss Myra Jennings, with her train bearers at the Gorsedd held at Bude in 1971.

The conclusion of the Second World War signalled general celebration and rejoicing in Bude. Here we see one of the children's Victory Parties held at the Grammar School.

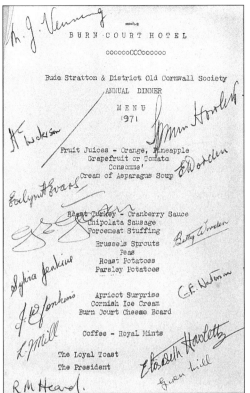

Bude Old Cornwall Society Dinner, 1971, menu and signatures (top left). The Bude Old Cornwall Society Banner (top right) was designed by Mr Stuart Thorn. It was laboriously and beautifully worked by Angela Howlett, daughter of the Howletts, who did so much for the Old Cornwall Society.

The Bude branch of the Old Cornwall Society emerged by resolution at a public meeting held in the Council Chambers in November 1961. The founding committee consisted of Mesdames Sweet, Gard, Mill, Savage and Jewel. The male members were Messrs Burrow, Luke, Heard (AC) Howlett and Ball. Mr Ball was elected chairman and Mr Spencer Howlett hon. secretary, a position he held with distinction for many years.

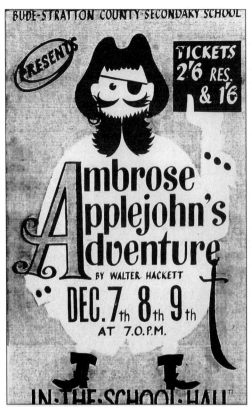

To the left is the poster for Stratton County Secondary School's annual Christmas Play in 1955. The stage designs were by Mr Ian Fraser, art master, and the sets were made by the pupils under the guidance of their woodwork master Mr Lloyd Sweet. Miss Betty Newman cast and directed the play. The standard attained was extremely high and the evenings were always a sell out! Below is a scene from the play. Amongst the members of the cast on stage are: Tim Higham, Margaret Luxton, Maureen Aunger and Jennifer Jollife.

The Wesleyan Church was built near the Causeway in 1880. The stone laying ceremony of the Sunday School took place on Whit Sunday 1910.

A very solemn looking group of boys and girls with their teachers from Stratton School, way back in 1905 – dressed and marshalled for the occasion.

Visitors to Bude come from far and wide. This one waiting at the bus stop came in 1973 complete with dog and mobile luggage carrier, but whether he was allowed on the bus is not recorded!

The Donkey Derby, organised by the Round Table in 1970, was won by Des Gregory, seen here. From the expressions of the participants the triumph appears to be mutual!

Six
Bude's Neighbours

Stratton occupies a south facing hillside above the river Neet about 2 miles to the east of Bude. This ancient settlement lies along the route of the prehistoric ridgeway into Cornwall. Historically it has mention in the will of Alfred the Great and 'Stratone' figures in the Domesday Survey of 1087. The ancient manor of Stratton was divided at the end of the twelfth century into two smaller manors, Binhamy and Efford. Binhamy became the home of the Blanchminster family, after whom the charity was named, whilst Efford came into the hands of the Arundells of Trerice in the early fifteenth century by marriage treaty. For many years it was the principal town in the Hundred which bore its name. However, from about the middle of the nineteenth century it has declined rapidly into the sleepy but attractive residential backwater we know today.

A splendid watercolour sketch by Ian Fraser of Leat Cottages, now demolished. The Leat led water from the River Neet to Howard Mill.

Fore Street, Stratton, in about 1890, and 'Tree Hill' with the Kings Arms on the right, leads up to The Tree Inn and Maiden Street. This was the old road to Bideford.

The Bay Tree Inn is in the foreground with Union Hill and the road to Bude straight ahead. Note that there were no houses on the skyline! These pictures were taken virtually from the same spot, facing roughly east and west.

Some of these picturesque cottages in Maiden Street were demolished to make way for a Methodist chapel around 1900.

Many will remember Heard's grocery shop in lower Stratton, near the Kings Arms corner. Mr John Heard is seen here outside the grocer's shop founded by Mr Sam Leach .

School children standing outside Leat Cottages on the bank of the River Neet, in about 1904. In the background is the old tannery.

During the First World War Stratton was a collecting point for horses required by the Army. Some of the poor beasts seen here are blissfully unaware of what fate had in store!

This cottage, one of the Leat cottages, known as 'Bonney's Cottage', was the home of Arthur Moyse the town barber. It is now demolished.

These ancient premises, which stood in front of the church, were demolished about 1895. The war memorial now stands on this site.

A group of prominent Stratton men in front of a shop shortly to be demolished. The church is behind. Masses of notices adorning the walls seem to indicate that the building was unoccupied but the area was a natural meeting place for townsfolk.

Despite its proximity to the church, the name refers to the manor of Sanctuary held by Launceston Priory until the Dissolution, when it was annexed to the Duchy.

THE SQUARE, WEEK ST MARY.

The Square, Week St Mary. Once a Saxon borough, but now a quiet and unassuming village, Week St Mary lies about seven miles south of Bude. It was from here that a sixteenth century shepherdess, Thomasina Bonaventure, was taken off to London by a rich wool merchant whom she subsequently married. On his death she remarried twice, her third husband becoming Lord Mayor of London. As a widow she returned to her native village with a vast fortune and devoted her time and money to good works in the local community. She is buried beside her third husband at St Mary Woolnoth in the city of London.

In February 1935, Week St Mary suffered a sudden and violent thunder storm that wreaked havoc locally. The church was badly damaged, losing a pinnacle from the tower and a considerable amount of debris penetrated the roof. It was almost a year before full worship could be resumed there.

Left: Morwenstowe; Robert Stephen Hawker was born in Stratton in 1804. An idiosyncratic churchman, poet and reformer, he was vicar of the parish for over forty years. The story of these exciting and often turbulent years is told by S. Baring-Gould in his famous book *The Vicar of Morwenstow*. Right: The porch and the Norman doorway in 1920 still clearly reveal their ancient origin after nine centuries, but the church at Morwenstowe has many other points of interest, both architectural and historical.

Whilst supervising the building of his new vicarage at Morwenstowe, Hawker lived in this cottage in the peace of Coombe Valley just north of Bude. It is said that the window of Hawker's study was so constructed that it threw the shadow of a cross onto one of the walls.

Revd R.S. Hawker standing outside his famous vicarage with his second wife and daughter. The stacks of the four chimneys were designed as replicas of the towers of churches with which Hawker had been previously associated. A fifth chimney was built in the shape of his mother's tomb.

Interior of the church. There are suggestions that this fascinating church was built on the site of an ancient Saxon settlement. Clear traces of Norman work can be seen in the north arcade but other indications suggest a Saxon religious influence, eg. the font. The picture was taken before the chancel screen was erected.

Millook, a small coastal settlement to the south of Bude, once boasted a water mill. The 'splash' in the late 1880s has now been replaced by a solid and respectable stone bridge. Tracts of the coastline north and south of Crackington Haven, which include Millook, were donated to the National Trust to commemorate the Battle of Britain in 1940 and to retain the memory of those gallant air crews who successfully countered the German menace.

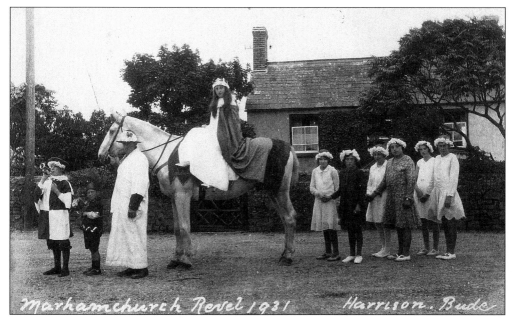

Marhamchurch, south east of Bude on the old canal, has another interesting church. It is dedicated to St Marwenne who emigrated to Cornwall from South Wales in the fifth century, founding a religious settlement. Her day, 12 August, is marked each year by a Revel, as seen here.

Below: Marhamchurch. The old two storey church house near the lych gate was removed in 1882 and a war memorial now stands near the site. The north of the square has also been considerably rebuilt. Behind the tree, long gone, a school once formed part of the site but two of the original cottages remain and can still be seen today. The church house door frame was moved to the school.

Widemouth. Although the Salt House at Widemouth still stands today, the road seen in front has long since disappeared into the sea and a modern highway is now situated some 100 yards inland to the east.

Poundstock. This two storied medieval church house is one of the oldest remaining in the county and one of the last still in active use. Its original function was partly social and partly religious. For a time it even served as the parish poorhouse.

Kilkhampton, 6 miles north of Bude and 600 ft above sea level, boasts a hybrid title in which an old Cornish name has been latched on to an English termination. The village too bears vestiges of a Celtic hamlet later converted to a nucleated settlement surrounded by open field systems. It boasts also a well defined site of a Norman motte and bailey castle, whilst the church, dedicated to St James, with its Norman south doorway is typical of the Cornish medieval period. It has a fine wagon roof and many quite superb bench ends, and the window traceries probably date to the fifteenth and sixteenth centuries. Kilkhampton was once a staging post on the northern stagecoach 'runs' from Bude. Above is The Square in 1906, and although the general outline has changed little, it has acquired a war memorial and car park. The freedom to roam in it certainly has gone. Below, the Bideford coach leaves the London Inn on it's northward run at the turn of the century, closely observed by an 'arm of the law'.

Kilkhampton School in 1936, with Miss Grace Stanbury in charge.

Kilkhampton School Concert in 1936 was devoted to animations of several familiar nursery rhymes. Ivor Potter, (now a well known Kilkhampton figure) is at the end of the row dressed as a plate - but we wonder where was the spoon? From the left: Betty Heard, Herbert Paragan, Bill Braund, John Hallett, Kathie Jordan, Freda Collins and Ivor Potter.

The Thynnes, who inherited all the Grenville Cornish properties, built themselves a fine home at Kilkhampton calling it Penstowe (upper Stowe), in 1862. This picture shows the Conservative Party Garden Fete of 1928, held in the grounds, to which all members of staff, indoor and out, were 'invited'. Bill Curtis, Bill White, Fred Rogers, Leslie White, Ron Jollife, Herbert Jollife, E. Mills, Harold Kinsman, William Routley and Arthur Braund are seen here.

The 1953 Fairy Queen, Janet Cornish, attended by Helen French and Margaret Wickett, disembarks from her regal coach surrounded by the regalia of her office in the centre of Kilkhampton.

Violet Burrows with her bucket, seen drawing water from the pump in Higher Square in about 1930.

Before the First World War there were two active blacksmiths premises in Kilkhampton. The picture shows Fulfords, the larger of the two.

The Parish Church of Kilkhampton is dedicated to St James, whose day, 25 July, was set aside for local celebrations. In this 1900 picture, taken from the church tower looking south, one can see the triumphal arch built across the main road south. Hardly a possibility today!

Rosemont Cottages at the approach to the church, seen here in 1952, incorporated materials from the Earl of Bath's mansion at Stowe which was demolished in 1739. The cottages themselves were removed in 1956 and the site now forms a car park.

The Grenvilles of Stowe. This is a picture of the great Sir Richard Grenville the hero of the *Revenge* which was sunk by superior Spanish forces off the Azores in 1591. The story of this gallant action is now a legend of Naval history and the subject of a book by A.L. Rowse.

The Grenville family, who claimed Norman origin, were considerable landowners in north Cornwall. They rose to political prominence in the reigns of the Tudors and Stuarts. We see the interior of the family vault in Kilkhampton Churchyard when it was unceremoniously breached in 1990 by an unfortunate workman tending the church exterior and an earth subsidence dumped him into the chamber below! John and Vivian Trewin can be seen exploring its interior. The mark on the wall indicates an earlier flooding. The remnants of Grenville pride and property in Kilkhampton were finally dispersed at the great sale which followed sometime after the death of Mrs Constance Thynne at the age 90, in 1961.